"Partition Suits in India: A Complete Guide"

Understand, Draft, and File with Confidence

NARAYANA SWAMY .R

Advocate Karnataka

NARAYANASWAMY.R

ACKNOWLEDGEMENTS

I am deeply grateful to the people who have been a constant source of inspiration, support, and guidance throughout my journey.

First and foremost, I dedicate this work to my beloved father, the late **Rangappa M.K.**, and my mother, **Lakshminarasamma**, whose unwavering values, sacrifices, and encouragement have been the foundation of my personal and professional life. Their teachings have been the guiding light that has carried me through every challenge.

I extend my heartfelt thanks to my brother, **Shivashankara**, your sacrifices and unwavering support have been my pillars of strength. I am forever grateful for your steadfast presence in my life

To my father-in-law, **Narayanappa M.V.**, and my mother-in-law, **Rathnamma**, I am indebted for their enduring faith in me and for the warmth and stability they bring to our family. Their kindness and belief in my work have been invaluable.

To my wife, **Gowthami MN**, my constant source of strength, patience, and understanding. Her support has been unwavering, and her sacrifices have allowed me the time and space necessary to bring this book to fruition. Words cannot fully capture my gratitude for her.

To my children, **Akiranandan** and **Aadhya**, who are my inspiration and motivation. Their smiles and curiosity remind me each day of the importance of passing down knowledge and values, and I hope this work serves as a part of that legacy.

A special acknowledgment goes to my mentor and senior advocate in the High Court, **Shrihari K.**, who has imparted invaluable wisdom, morals, and professional guidance. His teachings have left a lasting impression on my approach to the law and advocacy.

I would also like to thank my mentor, well wisher, **Chandbasha M.**, for his insightful discussions and unwavering encouragement throughout this journey. your guidance and wisdom have been instrumental in shaping my path.

This book is a culmination of the support, wisdom, and encouragement of all these incredible individuals. Thank you for being part of this journey.

Preface

The law of partition in India is a subject that touches on both personal and social aspects of family structure, property rights, and inheritance. As a practice deeply rooted in Indian culture, the concept of partition has always been fundamental in determining the distribution of ancestral properties. This book, Understanding Partition Suits: A Practical Guide to Claiming Ancestral Property Rights in India, is intended to provide clear, accessible insights into the legal principles governing partition suits and to guide individuals, practitioners, and law students through the complexities of these claims.

Partition suits arise from disputes over ancestral or joint family properties, where co-owners seek division to secure their individual shares. Rooted in Hindu and Muslim personal laws, as well as statutory laws like the Hindu Succession Act, partition law seeks to balance respect for family relationships with the legal rights of individuals to inherit and possess their share of family property. This book explores these legal frameworks in detail, clarifying how partition suits operate and the practical steps needed to pursue rightful inheritance.

Throughout the chapters, we delve into key topics, such as establishing one's right to ancestral property, understanding joint family structures, drafting legal notices, preparing partition suits, and gathering the necessary documents. Real-life scenarios are provided to illustrate the concepts and procedural nuances, making this book an invaluable resource for those involved in or preparing for partition-related legal proceedings.

The goal of this book is to simplify complex legal concepts and procedures, empowering readers to make informed decisions about claiming ancestral property. By bridging theoretical knowledge with practical applications, we hope to provide clarity on partition suits and equip readers with the tools necessary to navigate this intricate area of law confidently.

Narayanaswamy.R

Advocate, Karnataka

Table of contents

INTRODUCTION TO PARTITION SUITS IN INDIA

In India, the concept of a partition suit holds immense significance within the framework of family and property laws. A partition suit is a legal remedy available to co-owners or co-parceners seeking to divide their jointly owned or inherited property, ensuring that each person receives their rightful share. This legal route is often invoked due to disputes among family members or co-owners, where consensual division becomes challenging. With roots embedded in both Hindu and Muslim personal laws, as well as the general civil procedure, partition suits address complexities related to ancestral and self-acquired property, co-parcenary rights, and the rights of minors and women in property distribution.

The journey through a partition suit involves navigating intricate legal issues, including identifying heirs, valuing properties, calculating shares, and obtaining possession rights. Notably, it also requires understanding statutory provisions, landmark judgments, and procedural nuances of Indian law, especially under the Civil Procedure Code (CPC). For anyone entangled in or studying this area, a well-rounded understanding of these elements is crucial.

PARTITION: SOME INSIGHTS

Partition within the Hindu Undivided Family (HUF) framework is a significant legal process that leads to the separation of coparcenary property, thereby ending the joint family status. Derived from the term 'partition,' which means to divide or separate, this legal process formally breaks the collective ownership of property within a Hindu undivided family. The partition ensures that each coparcener (a family member entitled to an inheritance) receives their rightful share of property, marking a clear line between joint and individual ownership.

In Hindu law, the law of succession and partition of Hindu Undivided Family (HUF) property is governed by two primary schools: Mitakshara and Dayabhaga. These schools represent the foundation of Hindu family law in India, and although they share some common principles, they have distinct differences regarding inheritance rights, partition mechanisms, and the classification of property. Let's explore each school comprehensively.

1. The Mitakshara School

The Mitakshara School of Hindu law is widely practiced across most parts of India, except for a few regions where Dayabhaga is followed (primarily Bengal and Assam). It is one of the oldest schools of Hindu law, deriving its name from the Sanskrit commentary called Mitakshara, written by Vijnaneshwara, an ancient scholar.

Key Characteristics of the Mitakshara School

1. Doctrine of Survivorship:

- Under Mitakshara law, a key principle is survivorship, where property passes not by inheritance but by the rule of survivorship within the coparcenary. When a male member of a Hindu Undivided Family (HUF) dies, his share does not pass to his heirs; instead, it devolves upon the other living male coparceners.

- The property remains undivided as long as the family continues as an HUF, and shares are not separated until there is a partition.

2. Concept of Coparcenary and Ancestral Property:

- The Mitakshara school distinguishes between ancestral property and self-acquired property.

- Ancestral property is property inherited from one's father, grandfather, or great-grandfather, and forms a joint family property in which every male coparcener has a birthright.

- A coparcenary is a smaller body within the HUF consisting of the male members (now also daughters, per amendments) up to four generations from the common ancestor.

3. Coparcenary Rights by Birth:

- In Mitakshara law, sons (and now daughters, due to the 2005 amendment in Hindu Succession Act) acquire a right in the ancestral property by birth.

- This right by birth distinguishes Mitakshara from Dayabhaga law, where rights arise only upon the death of the father.

4. Partition Mechanism:

- A coparcener can demand partition of the HUF property, which means dividing the joint family property into specific shares, thus ending the joint status of the family regarding that property.

- Partition can either be total (covering all property) or partial (covering some parts), and once done, it cannot be reversed. Upon partition, each coparcener receives his share, and if there are minor children, their interests are represented by the guardian.

5. Share Allocation:

- During partition, the shares of coparceners vary based on the family members at the time of division.

- For instance, if a coparcener has sons, his share will be divided with his sons at the time of partition, which could impact the distribution of shares among the rest of the family.

Example of Mitakshara System

Imagine a family consisting of a father, his two sons, and one grandson from the eldest son. Under Mitakshara law, all three generations—father, sons, and grandson—form a coparcenary and each has a right to demand partition of the ancestral property. If the father dies, his share in the coparcenary property passes by survivorship to the remaining coparceners (sons and grandson), not by inheritance.

2. The Dayabhaga School

The Dayabhaga School is primarily followed in the regions of Bengal and Assam. It differs from Mitakshara in its approach to inheritance, partition, and the notion of coparcenary rights. The Dayabhaga system is based on the commentary Dayabhaga written by Jimutavahana, another ancient scholar.

Key Characteristics of the Dayabhaga School

1. Doctrine of Inheritance by Succession:

- In Dayabhaga law, the concept of survivorship does not apply. Instead, property devolves by inheritance. A coparcener's share is passed on to their heirs upon death, rather than to other coparceners.

- This creates a clear and independent right in the property only upon the death of the father or previous owner, differing significantly from the Mitakshara approach.

2. Rights Only Upon Father's Death:

- Unlike Mitakshara law, where children acquire an interest in the ancestral property by birth, in Dayabhaga law, children do not get any rights in the property until the father's death.

- This essentially means that the father has absolute control over the property, and sons/daughters have no automatic rights to it while he is alive.

3. Classification of Property:

- Under Dayabhaga, all property is treated as individual property during the lifetime of the owner, and there is no concept of ancestral property as seen in the Mitakshara system.

- Each family member's property is considered distinct and subject to inheritance upon their death, rather than a collective ownership within the coparcenary.

4. Partition:

- Partition in Dayabhaga law involves the division of property according to each heir's inherited rights rather than a division of joint family property by birthright.

- Since there are no birthrights in the property, partition only occurs after the death of the property holder, ensuring no share is predetermined by birth.

5. Share Allocation:

- Shares are determined based on the law of inheritance. For instance, if the father dies, his property is divided among his heirs as per the succession rules, and shares are not influenced by any co-ownership arrangement as seen in Mitakshara.

Example of Dayabhaga System

Suppose a father in Bengal has two sons and one daughter. While he is alive, he holds exclusive ownership of his property. Upon his death, each of his children inherits an equal share of his property according to succession rules. The sons or daughter do not have any claim on the property as long as the father is alive.

Major Differences Between Mitakshara and Dayabhaga Schools

The Mitakshara and Dayabhaga schools, two major schools of Hindu law, differ significantly in how they interpret rights, devolution, and control over property among family members.

Under the Mitakshara school, the right to ancestral property is granted by birth, which means that sons and daughters acquire an interest in the family property from the moment they are born. This school follows the principle of survivorship within the coparcenary, where property is passed on to surviving male members upon the death of a coparcener. Members in this system can demand partition of the family property at any time, with their control over it being shared among the coparcenary members, limiting individual autonomy over the property. Mitakshara law is practiced across most parts of India, except in Bengal and Assam.

Conversely, the Dayabhaga school provides that property rights are vested in heirs only upon the father's death, rather than by birth. Here, inheritance follows the principle of succession, with property being transferred to the legal heirs after the owner's death, as opposed to passing through survivorship. Partition under Dayabhaga law can only occur after the death of the property owner, granting the father absolute control over the property during his lifetime. This school of thought is specific to the regions of Bengal and Assam.

These distinctions impact how property rights are managed within families, influencing inheritance practices across various regions in India.

Impact of the Hindu Succession (Amendment) Act, 2005

With the amendment in 2005, daughters were granted coparcenary rights in HUF property, thus allowing them equal rights to ancestral property, similar to sons. This change primarily affects the Mitakshara system since it includes the concept of ancestral property and coparcenary rights by birth. In Dayabhaga, since rights only accrue after the death of the father, daughters inherit equal shares with sons in such cases without the need for coparcenary adjustments.

Conclusion

The two schools of Hindu law, Mitakshara and Dayabhaga, offer distinct frameworks for managing succession and partition of HUF property, with differences rooted in regional practices and interpretations of inheritance. The Mitakshara school emphasizes birthrights and joint ownership within a coparcenary, whereas Dayabhaga follows a model of inheritance upon death, preserving individual ownership while the head of the family is alive. Despite these differences, both systems have evolved with legal reforms, particularly with respect to gender equality, as seen in the 2005 amendment granting daughters equal rights in the HUF property. Understanding these schools is crucial for determining property rights and succession in Hindu family law, reflecting traditional legal interpretations balanced with modern statutory reforms.

THE LAW OF PARTITION: HINDU AND MUSLIM INSIGHTS EXPLAINED

1. Hindu Law

Partition under Hindu law is generally governed by the Hindu Succession Act, 1956, and is rooted in the concept of joint family property. The principles vary slightly between Mitakshara and Dayabhaga schools of Hindu law.

Types of Property:

- Joint Family Property: Property inherited from ancestors, shared among family members.

- Self-Acquired Property: Property acquired by an individual, which remains under personal ownership until expressly made part of the joint property.

Right to Partition:

- In a Hindu Joint Family (Hindu Undivided Family or HUF), co-parceners (typically male descendants) have a right to demand partition of the joint family property.

- The Hindu Succession (Amendment) Act, 2005, gave daughters equal rights as sons, making them co-parceners in the HUF.

Partition Process:

- A partition can occur by mutual consent or through a partition suit in court when members disagree on division.

- **Court processes involve:**

- Filing a partition suit by a co-parcener with a claim detailing the share they seek.

- Valuing the properties, verifying ancestral origin, and ensuring fair distribution based on shares of each co-parcener.

- Division can be by metes and bounds (physical division) or by sale and distribution of proceeds if physical division isn't feasible.

Effect of Partition:

- Upon partition, each co-parcener receives a specific share, ceasing the joint family status concerning the divided property.

- Partial partition (dividing only a part of the property) is also permissible, where specific assets are separated while others remain jointly held.

Female Co-parceners:

- The 2005 amendment ensures daughters are included in the partition as equal co-parceners, giving them the right to claim their share of the HUF property, even if born before 2005.

2. Muslim Law

Unlike Hindu law, Muslim law does not formally recognize joint family property or co-parcenary. Muslim law primarily adheres to the principle of individual ownership, and inheritance rather than partition regulates property rights.

Inheritance and Succession:

- Properties are divided among legal heirs according to personal law principles (Sunni or Shia laws), following inheritance rules after the owner's death.

- Muslim inheritance laws detail fixed shares for heirs (e.g., one-third or two-thirds), depending on the number of heirs and their relationship to the deceased.

Types of Heirs:

- **Sharers**: Close relatives such as spouses, parents, and children who have fixed shares in the property.

- **Residuaries**: Those who inherit the remaining property after sharers have received their portions.

- **Distant Kindred**: More distant relatives who may inherit only if no sharers or residuaries are present.

Partition Process in Muslim Law:

- Since properties are not considered joint family properties, partition suits under Muslim law typically arise only in cases of disputed inheritance.

- When disputes arise, a partition suit can be filed to ensure the rightful distribution as per each heir's share, especially when property has not been voluntarily divided post-death.

- Muslim law allows for the distribution of inheritance based on the doctrine of 'Taqseem' (division), and the court oversees the just allocation per legal shares.

Role of Will (Wasiyat):

- A Muslim can only will up to one-third of their property to non-heirs. The remaining two-thirds are subject to the standard inheritance rules unless consent for a larger will is obtained from all heirs.

Key Differences: Hindu vs. Muslim Law in Partition

In Hindu law, the concept of joint family property, or Hindu Undivided Family (HUF) property, is recognized, which allows family members to own property collectively under a single legal entity. This concept is not present in Muslim law, where each family member holds individual ownership over their assets without the formation of a joint family property structure.

When it comes to partition rights, Hindu law allows co-parceners—members who are entitled to a share in the ancestral property—to demand partition. This right extends to daughters as well, granting them equal status as sons in family property matters. In contrast, under Muslim law, partition is typically facilitated through inheritance rather than by direct demand from the heirs. The distribution of property, once a family member passes away, is conducted according to predetermined shares set by Islamic inheritance laws.

Hindu law bases distribution on equal shares for sons and daughters within an HUF structure, ensuring all family members receive a fair portion. Muslim law, however, operates on fixed shares for each legal heir as mandated by religious doctrines, leaving little flexibility in the division process.

With respect to wills, Hindu law allows a property owner to will their entire self-acquired property to any chosen individual(s), as there are no legal restrictions on how much of their property can be allocated through a will. Muslim law, however, restricts this freedom; an individual may only will up to one-third of their property to someone outside the legal heirs without obtaining the consent of these heirs.

In cases of dispute, courts under Hindu law ensure fair partition by verifying each co-parcener's share and overseeing the equitable distribution of assets. Under Muslim law, courts play a role in ensuring that the inheritance division follows Islamic inheritance laws correctly, aiming to uphold the set entitlements of each heir.

3. Partition Suit Filing Procedure:

For both Hindu and Muslim laws, a partition suit is typically initiated when heirs or co-parceners cannot agree on property division.

Conclusion

Understanding the unique approaches of Hindu and Muslim law toward partition is crucial to fair property division. Hindu law recognizes co-parcenary, allowing male and female heirs equal shares, while Muslim law's individual ownership model follows fixed inheritance laws. In both, courts play an essential role in settling disputes and ensuring justice based on religious principles and modern legal frameworks.

THE DYNAMICS OF HINDU FAMILY PARTITION: ELIGIBILITY, PROPERTY, AND DECREE ESSENTIALS

Partition in Hindu law transforms a joint family structure into distinct individual family units, marking the end of the collective identity and the beginning of individual nuclear families. For instance, when A and his sons, B and C, undergo partition, three separate families emerge for each member. This process, governed primarily by the Hindu Succession Act, 1956, and guided by the principles of the Mitakshara and Dayabhaga schools, involves key considerations in determining who is eligible for partition, what properties can be divided, and the role of third-party purchasers. Let's delve into the core aspects.

Persons Eligible to Seek Partition Under Hindu Succession Act, 1956

Under Hindu Succession Act, 1956, as amended in 2005, both male and female coparceners in a joint family possess the right to seek partition. The 2005 amendment notably recognized daughters as coparceners, giving them equal rights to property alongside sons, grandsons, and great-grandsons.

- Male Coparceners: Sons, grandsons, and great-grandsons hold a birthright in the joint family property and can demand partition at any time.

- Female Coparceners: Since the 2005 amendment, daughters enjoy the same coparcenary rights as sons. This right applies to daughters regardless of when they were born, provided they remain a part of the joint family.

- Minors: Both male and female minors can claim a share through their guardians, who may file a suit on their behalf.

Special Cases:

- After-born Sons: Sons conceived before partition but born after it can reopen partition to claim a share. Sons conceived and born after the partition are entitled only to their father's share and cannot reopen partition for their separate share.

- Illegitimate Sons: Limited rights, typically to maintenance, with inheritance rights depending on caste.

- Adopted Sons: Considered as born into the adoptive family; they have a right to demand partition as coparceners.

Nature of Property Liable for Partition with Reference to Coparcenary

The Hindu coparcenary property consists of assets that members inherit by birth, and only such properties are eligible for partition. Partition does not include:

- Joint Family Property: Generally, all properties acquired and owned by the family collectively are subject to division.

- Separate or Self-Acquired Property: This is not subject to partition unless voluntarily contributed to the coparcenary.

- Impartible Properties: Certain properties (e.g., family idols, religious assets, or those dedicated to religious purposes) cannot be partitioned.

- Properties of Unique Nature: Items like family idols, certain estate properties governed by primogeniture, and passages are often excluded to preserve their collective familial or religious importance.

- Movable vs. Immovable Property: Each coparcener is entitled to an equitable share, which may include both movable and immovable properties. When an exact division is impractical, financial compensation may be awarded to equalize distribution.

Status of Third-Party Purchasers

When a coparcener sells their undivided share, the purchaser may seek a partition to establish their separate share. However:

- Purchaser Rights: Third-party purchasers have rights limited to the undivided share of the seller and must file for a partition suit to claim possession.

- Karta's Authority: Only the Karta (family manager) can alienate coparcenary property without other members' consent, provided it is for legal necessity, estate benefit, or essential family obligations. Purchases by third parties from coparceners other than the Karta generally need coparceners' consent or court intervention to secure rights.

Preliminary, Final Decree & Mesne Profits in Partition Suits

1. Preliminary Decree: This decree determines the specific shares and rights of each coparcener but does not finalize the division. Once issued, it legally establishes parties' rights unless contested in appeal. For example, a court might decide that each member is entitled to a one-third share in the family property.

2. Final Decree: The final decree concludes the partition by specifying exact property divisions. It builds on the preliminary decree's foundation and finalizes property allocation "by metes and bounds." After this decree, all disputes in the suit are resolved, establishing individual ownership of partitioned assets.

3. Mesne Profits: These are compensations owed by a party in wrongful possession to the rightful owner. Under Order XX Rule 12 of the Civil Procedure Code, 1908, mesne profits ensure that those who lost access to their property receive fair compensation for the wrongful occupancy period until possession is restored.

Case Laws Illustrating Partition Rights

1. Baljinder Singh v. Rattan Singh (2008): Established that a coparcener's gift of an undivided interest without the consent of other coparceners is void.

2. Beereddy Dasaratharami Reddy v. V. Manjunath (2021): Confirmed the Karta's right to sell joint family property for legal necessities.

3. Vineetha Sharma v. Rakesh Sharma (2020): Overruled prior case law, confirming daughters' rights to equal shares in coparcenary property regardless of their father's status at the amendment's enactment.

4. Kattukandi Edathil Krishnan v. Kattukandi Edathil Valsan (2022): Reinforced the obligation of courts to proactively proceed with final decree proceedings after a preliminary decree in partition suits

INHERITANCE UNDER A WILL:ESSENTIALS

Inheritance in India can occur through two main avenues: personal laws and wills. A will or testament represents a legal declaration through which an individual, known as the testator, formally outlines their wishes regarding the distribution of their property or estate upon their death. The purpose of a will is to ensure that the testator's assets pass to the intended beneficiaries as per their explicit instructions, rather than following standard rules of inheritance under personal laws.

Key Aspects of a Will

1. **Definition and Purpose**: A will is a formal document wherein the testator specifies how their assets—such as property, investments, and personal belongings—should be distributed after their death. By making a will, the testator gains control over the disposition of their self-acquired or individually owned property, thereby providing clarity and preventing potential conflicts among heirs.

2. **Role of the Executor**: In a will, the testator typically appoints an executor, a trusted individual responsible for managing and

overseeing the distribution of assets as per the will's instructions. The executor's duties include collecting the testator's assets, paying any debts or taxes, and ensuring that beneficiaries receive their designated inheritance smoothly and in compliance with the testator's wishes.

3. Scope of Property Covered by a Will:

- A will is applicable only to the self-acquired property or separate property of the testator. This means that the testator has the authority to distribute assets they independently own or have acquired through personal effort or investment.

- However, for ancestral property—property inherited through family lineage—the rules differ. Ancestral property is generally distributed according to inheritance laws outlined in the Hindu Succession Act, 1956 or other relevant personal laws, rather than the testator's personal wishes. This legal distinction aims to preserve family property for rightful heirs, often restricting the testator's ability to include ancestral assets in their will.

4. **Execution and Validity**: For a will to be legally effective, it must adhere to specific formalities, including the testator's voluntary consent, signature, and typically the presence of witnesses. Any undue influence or lack of mental capacity can render a will invalid.

Benefits of Creating a Will

- Prevention of Disputes: A well-drafted will reduces ambiguity in property distribution, helping prevent disputes among heirs.

- Customized Distribution: Unlike inheritance laws, which may distribute assets equally among legal heirs, a will allows the testator to make tailored bequests, providing for family members or dependents in unique ways.

- Ease of Transfer: With an appointed executor to manage the estate, the process of inheritance becomes streamlined, avoiding potential legal hurdles or delays.

Conclusion

A will is an essential estate-planning tool, especially for individuals who wish to exercise control over the distribution of their self-acquired assets. By drafting a will, individuals can safeguard their wishes and reduce the likelihood of disputes among their heirs. However, understanding the distinction between self-acquired and ancestral property is crucial, as the distribution of ancestral assets follows prescribed legal succession laws that may not align with the testator's personal intentions. Thus, for a seamless and conflict-free inheritance process, creating a clear and legally sound will is indispensable.

SELF-ACQUIRED PROPERTY: A GUIDE TO EFFECTIVE PARTITIONING

In India, the rules governing the partition of self-acquired property are distinct from those concerning ancestral property. Unlike ancestral property, where family members inherently hold a claim, self-acquired property belongs solely to the individual who acquired it, and only they have the absolute authority over its disposal or division. Indian courts, through various judgments, have helped clarify these provisions, emphasizing the limited rights of children and grandchildren over such property.

Key Judicial Interpretations on Self-Acquired Property

1. No Automatic Right of Claim by Children:

- In the landmark case of Sachin & Anr v. Jhabbu Lal & Anr, the court ruled that a son has no inherent right to claim ownership of his parent's self-acquired property unless he can provide concrete evidence of having contributed financially or otherwise toward acquiring the property. Simply put, children cannot demand ownership or partition of their parents' self-acquired property as a matter of right.

- The court further observed that while a son may be allowed to use or reside in the property with the parent's permission, this does not create any legal entitlement to the property. Parents have the discretion to allow or disallow their children to live in their self-acquired property without any legal obligation.

2. No Partition Rights During the Parent's Lifetime:

- In a 2019 judgment, the Delhi High Court reaffirmed that self-acquired property cannot be partitioned during the lifetime of the owner (for instance, the father). This means that even though the son may desire a share, he cannot demand or enforce a partition while the parent who owns the property is alive. The ruling reinforces that self-acquired property is the exclusive property of the individual who acquired it, preserving their rights to retain or distribute it as they see fit.

3. Hindu Succession Act, 1956:

- According to the Hindu Succession Act, 1956, self-acquired property of a parent does not automatically become joint family property or coparcenary property. Consequently, children do not inherit any share in the self-acquired property of their parents unless the parent chooses to pass it down through a will or gift.

- However, if a son or any other family member can demonstrate through evidence that they contributed to the acquisition of the self-acquired property, they may be eligible to claim a share based on their proven contribution. This exception ensures that any substantial contribution made by family members toward acquiring or developing self-acquired property is recognized.

4. Rights of Grandchildren:

- Notably, grandchildren do not have any automatic right to claim their grandfather's self-acquired property. Just as sons and daughters hold no legal claim, grandchildren too are barred from demanding a partition or share in self-acquired property unless it has been bequeathed to them through a will or gift.

Effect of a Will or Gift

The owner of self-acquired property has the freedom to bequeath it as they wish, including to third parties, by way of a will or a gift deed. In such cases:

- If a parent, for example, decides to transfer their self-acquired property to a third party, neither their children nor grandchildren can legally challenge this transfer.

- The will or gift deed reflects the parent's exclusive decision regarding their self-acquired property, making it binding and enforceable.

Conclusion

In summary, the legal stance on the partition of self-acquired property is rooted in the principle of individual ownership and discretion. Sons, daughters, and grandchildren do not possess any inherent right to claim such property; they may do so only if the parent chooses to allocate it to them. This protection ensures that self-acquired property remains at the absolute discretion of the owner, who can decide its future based on their preferences or through testamentary documents such as a will or gift deed. This framework not only upholds the autonomy of property owners but also encourages orderly and undisputed inheritance practices.

SPLITTING THE HERITAGE: THE ESSENTIALS OF ANCESTRAL PROPERTY PARTITION

Ancestral property is defined as property that has been inherited through a family lineage for up to three generations. The laws governing the partition and inheritance of ancestral property in India are primarily outlined in the Hindu Succession Act and were significantly amended by the Hindu Succession (Amendment) Act, 2005. This amendment brought about crucial changes, particularly in recognizing the rights of daughters as coparceners, thus promoting gender equality in inheritance.

Historical Context

Prior to the 2005 amendment, Hindu law recognized only males as coparceners, limiting the rights of female heirs in matters of ancestral property. However, the amendment fundamentally altered this framework, allowing daughters to have equal rights as sons in ancestral property. This shift not only aligned with contemporary views on gender equality but also reinforced the principle that both sons and daughters should have equal rights in family property.

Rights of Coparceners

1. Automatic Rights Upon Birth:

- Under the amended provisions, both sons and daughters acquire their rights in ancestral property automatically at birth. This means that as soon as a child is born into the family, they hold a legal claim to a share of the ancestral property.

2. Demand for Partition:

- A son or daughter can demand a partition of the ancestral property at any point during their father's lifetime. The only condition for claiming their share is to prove their relationship and succession rights through evidence. This empowers children to assert their rights and seek equitable distribution of family property.

3. Equal Shares:

- In the case of partition, all coparceners (both male and female) are entitled to an equal share in the ancestral property. This ensures fairness and equality in distribution, reflecting the principle that all descendants have an equal stake in their family heritage.

In the landmark judgment of Vineeta Sharma v. Rakesh Sharma, the Supreme Court of India reinforced the rights of daughters to inherit ancestral property on par with male heirs, further legitimizing their status as joint legal heirs.

Intestate vs. Testamentary Succession

- Testamentary Succession: This refers to the distribution of a deceased person's property as per their will. Under testamentary succession, the testator has the discretion to bequeath his self-acquired property to any individual, including sons, daughters, or third parties. The existence of a will supersedes the automatic inheritance rights typically associated with intestate succession.

- Intestate Succession: This occurs when an individual dies without leaving a will. In such cases, the rules of intestate succession apply, determining how ancestral property is to be divided among legal heirs. Under intestate succession, the law mandates equal distribution among all Class I heirs, which now includes daughters, thanks to the 2005 amendment.

Filing a Partition Suit

In situations where disputes arise over the division of ancestral property and cannot be resolved amicably among heirs, parties may resort to legal action. A partition suit can be filed in a civil court to seek a judicial decree for partitioning the ancestral property. The court will then adjudicate the matter, ensuring that each rightful heir receives their due share based on the legal provisions.

Conclusion

The partition of ancestral property in India is a critical area of law that has evolved significantly, particularly with the recognition of daughters as coparceners. The Hindu Succession (Amendment) Act, 2005, has paved the way for equitable rights, ensuring that all heirs—regardless of gender—are treated fairly in the distribution of family property. Understanding these rules is essential for individuals navigating the complexities of inheritance and property rights, and for resolving disputes that may arise in the context of family assets.

INHERITANCE INSIGHT: RULES FOR DIVIDING PROPERTY AFTER A FATHER'S DEATH

When a father passes away, the distribution of his property among his legal heirs is governed by inheritance laws, specifically the Hindu Succession Act, 1956 for Hindus. According to these laws, all legal heirs under Class I are entitled to an equal share in the deceased's property if he dies intestate (without a will). Class I heirs include the deceased's sons, daughters, widow, and in some cases, the mother, as well as other specified heirs. The law ensures equitable distribution of assets among these legal heirs, reflecting a fundamental shift toward gender equality in inheritance.

Equal Rights of Sons and Daughters

Under the Hindu Succession Act, both sons and daughters are considered Class I heirs. They are entitled to an equal share in the father's property, thereby ensuring that gender does not influence inheritance rights.

Illustration:

Consider a scenario where Ravi, the father, passes away, leaving behind two sons (Raj and Mohan), one daughter (Priya), and his wife (Suman). If Ravi dies intestate, his property will be divided equally among his legal heirs: Raj, Mohan, Priya, and Suman.

Thus, each will receive a 1/4th share of the property. This rule applies regardless of whether the property is ancestral or self-acquired, as long as Ravi dies without a will.

Rights of Stepson and Stepdaughter

A stepson or stepdaughter does not have any inherent legal right to claim a share in the father's property through intestate succession. According to the Hindu Succession Act, the term "daughter" does not include stepdaughters, and similarly, stepsons are not recognized as legal heirs in the absence of a will.

- Inheritance Rights: For a stepson or stepdaughter to inherit a share of the property, the father must specifically name them in a will, bequeathing a portion of his estate in their favor. Otherwise, they cannot claim any right to the property under the standard inheritance laws.

Key Points in Property Distribution:

1. Class I Heirs' Rights: Only the legal heirs recognized under Class I, such as sons, daughters, and the widow, can claim an automatic share in the property after the father's death if he dies intestate.

2. Equal Share: The property is divided equally among all eligible Class I heirs, ensuring fair and unbiased distribution.

3. Exclusion of Stepchildren: Stepson and stepdaughter are excluded from claiming a share in the property by default. They

are only entitled to inherit if explicitly included in a will made by the father.

Summary

The Hindu Succession Act provides a clear framework for distributing a father's property among his legal heirs, ensuring fairness and equality among sons and daughters. While Class I heirs automatically receive equal shares, stepsons and stepdaughters are excluded unless the father explicitly bequeaths a share to them through a will. This structure promotes equitable inheritance practices, honoring both traditional and contemporary principles of family and property law.

WHEN A FATHER GIFTS A PROPERTY

When a father gifts property to his son, the nature of that property changes significantly. Such gifted property is not classified as ancestral property. Consequently, while the son is entitled to claim his share in the property gifted to his father by his grandfather, it is essential to understand how the gift affects ownership rights.

Classification of Property

1. Gifted Property:

- When a father transfers property to his son as a gift, that property becomes the son's self-acquired property. This classification means that the property is now solely owned by the son, and his children (the grandchildren of the father) do not have any legal claim to it. This is a fundamental distinction because it contrasts with ancestral property, which can have rights that extend to grandchildren.

2. Ancestral Property:

- For property to be classified as ancestral, there must be clear intention from the grandfather (the father of the father) to declare it as such. Without this intention, the property remains self-acquired, and the typical rights associated with ancestral property do not apply.

Laws Governing Partition Suits

In India, the laws that govern the partition of property, especially in the context of Hindu families, are rooted in both statutory law and procedural rules:

1. Hindu Succession Act, 1956:

- This Act provides the framework for inheritance and succession in Hindu families, outlining the rights of heirs in terms of property distribution.

2. Code of Civil Procedure, 1860:

- Specific provisions relevant to partition suits are included in this Code, such as:

- Section 54: Relates to the sale of immovable property.

- Order 20 Rule 18: Governs the determination of shares in a partition suit.

- Order 26 Rule 13 & 14: Addresses the appointment of a commissioner to partition property.

Eligibility for Filing a Partition Suit

The eligibility to file a partition suit is generally governed by certain principles, particularly concerning coparceners and legal heirs:

1. Non-Coparceners:

- Non-coparceners, individuals who do not hold a stake in the coparcenary property, typically do not possess the right to demand a share in the property through a partition suit.

2. Aliens and Purchasers:

- An alienee (the person to whom property is transferred) or a purchaser of property through court execution has the right to demand a partition. However, they can only seek a partial partition, limited to the property in which they have an interest.

3. Legal Heirs:

- In situations where there are multiple legal heirs, if all parties do not agree to participate in the partition suit, any one or more of the heirs can file the suit on behalf of others. This ensures that the process can proceed even in cases of disagreement among heirs.

4. Legal Notice Requirement:

In India, a legal notice is generally not a mandatory requirement to initiate a partition suit, but it is often recommended as a prudent step before proceeding with litigation. Here's an in-depth look at why serving a legal notice before a partition suit is customary, and the situations in which it might or might not be required.

1. Legal Requirement vs. Good Practice

- No Absolute Requirement: Under the Code of Civil Procedure, 1908 (CPC), no specific provision mandates that a legal notice must be served before filing a partition suit. Unlike certain cases under Section 80 of the CPC, where a notice is compulsory (such as suits against the government or public officers), a partition suit falls under personal and family disputes, so the initiation does not strictly require pre-litigation notice.

- Good Practice for Settlement: Serving a notice allows the parties to attempt to resolve the matter amicably without involving the courts. In family matters, courts tend to encourage amicable settlements. A legal notice can help establish intentions clearly, enabling co-heirs or co-owners to discuss the terms and explore the possibility of a mutual partition.

2. Purpose and Benefits of a Legal Notice in Partition Suits

- Clarifies Intent and Claims: A legal notice serves as formal communication to co-owners or family members, indicating the intention to claim one's share in the ancestral or joint family property. It outlines the basis of the claim, the details of the property, and the specific share sought by the party issuing the notice.

- Sets the Stage for Negotiation: If there is no severe dispute but only a lack of consensus among co-owners, a legal notice might encourage a mutual agreement without needing litigation. Such an outcome saves time, legal expenses, and maintains familial relationships.

- Documented Evidence of Demand: Should the matter eventually reach court, a legal notice serves as evidence of an initial attempt at an amicable resolution. Courts, especially in family disputes, may consider this as a positive attempt to avoid litigation, which can sometimes influence the court's stance on cost orders or procedural leniencies.

3. Situations Where Legal Notice is Highly Advisable

- Property in Joint Ownership: If the property is held in joint ownership or there is no clear demarcation of shares, serving a notice clarifies the intent of the plaintiff (person initiating the suit) and often helps co-owners understand the exact share being sought.

- Pending Disputes or Hostility Among Co-Owners: Where family disputes or hostility already exist, a notice can formalize the demand for partition, clarifying the plaintiff's legal intent and detailing their proposed share. This may also prompt the defendants to negotiate or state their objections beforehand.

- Avoiding Allegations of Surprise or Bad Faith: In family property disputes, courts are sometimes sympathetic to parties who may feel blindsided by sudden litigation. Serving a legal notice counters potential claims that the plaintiff filed the suit in bad faith or without adequate warning.

4. Cases Where Notice May Not Be Necessary

- Urgency Due to Risk of Alienation: If the plaintiff suspects that the other co-owners or family members may alienate, sell, or transfer the property to third parties before partition, filing a suit directly with an injunction application might be preferable. Here, a legal notice may delay proceedings and give time to co-owners to transfer the property, risking the plaintiff's share.

- Risk of Property Loss or Dilapidation: Where the property's condition is deteriorating or at risk of being damaged, plaintiffs may proceed directly with a suit to obtain immediate relief, particularly if they seek court orders to safeguard the property.

5. Legal Notice Content for a Partition Suit

A well-drafted legal notice for a partition suit should include the following:

- Introduction of the Sender and Co-Heirs: Details of the sender's relationship with other co-heirs, outlining their connection to the property.

- Description of the Ancestral Property: Full details, including location, nature, and any specific identifiers, like survey numbers or plot details.

- Legal Right and Share Claimed: A clear statement of the sender's legal entitlement, detailing their share based on succession laws or family arrangements.

- Request for Amicable Partition: A request for an amicable partition of the property or for division based on mutually acceptable terms, with a reasonable deadline for response.

- Consequence of Non-Compliance: A statement indicating the intent to initiate legal proceedings if no resolution is reached within the specified period.

6. Conclusion: Practical Necessity of a Legal Notice

In summary, while a legal notice is not legally mandated for partition suits, it is generally a wise and beneficial step. It strengthens the plaintiff's position by demonstrating an initial effort to settle the matter amicably, establishes clear communication, and minimizes the risk of unforeseen disputes during litigation. Moreover, courts in India often appreciate parties attempting alternative dispute resolution, making the notice an advantage for the plaintiff if the case proceeds to trial.

In conclusion, issuing a legal notice before filing a partition suit is a strategic approach that enhances the transparency, clarity, and potential goodwill of the partition proceedings, potentially saving time, legal costs, and familial relations.

Conclusion

The partition of property, especially in the context of gifted and ancestral property, involves complex legal principles governed by the Hindu Succession Act and procedural laws. Understanding the distinctions between self-acquired and ancestral property is crucial, particularly regarding the rights of sons and daughters. The eligibility to file a partition suit is primarily limited to coparceners and those with vested interests, ensuring that the legal process is fair and equitable. Engaging a legal professional is advisable for any coparcener or legal heir contemplating a partition suit, as navigating the intricacies of property law requires expertise to ensure compliance with all procedural requirements.

GET YOUR PAPERS IN ORDER: DOCUMENTS FOR PARTITION SUITS EXPLAINED

Filing a partition suit is a significant legal step that involves various documents to substantiate the claim. While there is no specific legal provision detailing every document required for a partition suit, certain essential documents are typically necessary to support the filing and establish the claimant's rights. Here's a comprehensive overview of the documents commonly required:

1. Title Deeds

The foremost document required when filing a partition suit is the certified copy or original copy of all title deeds of the property being claimed as ancestral. These documents serve as proof of ownership and are critical in establishing the legal rights of the claimants over the property. Without these deeds, it can be challenging to assert claims regarding the property in question.

2. Description of the Property

A comprehensive and appropriate description of the property is crucial when filing a partition suit. The description should include the following details:

- Area: The total area of the property must be clearly stated.

- Location: The specific location of the property should be mentioned, including the address.

- Survey Numbers: Relevant survey numbers that identify the property in land records must be included.

- Geographical Boundaries: Clear demarcation of the property boundaries is essential for the court's understanding of the extent of the property.

- Other Property Details: Any additional details relevant to the property that may support the claim should also be provided.

3. Market Valuation of the Property

A market valuation of the property is another important document required for filing a partition suit. This valuation helps ascertain the property's worth and can be conducted with the assistance of the concerned sub-registrar. The market value is significant, especially in determining the equitable distribution of property among co-owners.

4. Death Certificates

In cases where the partition involves inherited property, a death certificate of the claimant's grandparent or parent (whichever applies to the specific case) is required. These certificates serve as proof of death, which is vital in establishing the line of succession and the rights of the heirs. Death certificates can typically be obtained from the relevant municipal authorities.

5. Jurisdiction

It is important to note that the partition suit must be filed in the court having jurisdiction over the partition property. The specific court is usually determined by the location of the property and the legal provisions applicable to the case.

Conclusion

In summary, while there is flexibility regarding the specific documents required to file a partition suit, possessing the right foundational documents is crucial. Title deeds, property descriptions, market valuations, and death certificates form the core of the documentation needed to substantiate claims in a partition suit. Engaging legal expertise is essential to navigate the process effectively, ensuring that all necessary documents are gathered and submitted correctly.

LIMITATION FOR FILING A PARTITION SUIT IN INDIA

Overview

The limitation period for filing a partition suit in India does not follow a straightforward, fixed rule. Instead, it depends heavily on the nature of the property and the relationship between the co-sharers. Unlike other property-related suits, partition suits do not have a prescribed limitation period under Indian law. This flexible approach is based on the principle that a co-sharer always has the inherent right to seek partition whenever they no longer wish to retain a joint interest in the property.

Key Legal Principles

1. No Prescribed Limitation Period:

- Indian law does not specify a fixed period for filing a partition suit. The right to partition is viewed as an inherent right associated with co-ownership of property, creating a "running cause of action." This means that a co-sharer can seek partition at any time without being constrained by a rigid timeframe, as long as they hold a legitimate claim to the property. For instance, in the Mariyam Bibi W/o Hafijul Haq vs. Kutubuddin S/o Rojid Miya (Chhattisgarh) case, the court reiterated this concept, allowing co-sharers to claim their share whenever they choose not to keep it joint.

2. Running Cause of Action:

- In partition suits, the cause of action begins whenever a co-sharer decides to seek partition, granting flexibility to file a suit without immediate restrictions. For example, in Neelmani Singh vs. Tikka Brijinder Singh Bedi (Delhi), the court confirmed that unless a co-sharer expressly relinquishes their right to seek partition, they maintain the ability to initiate a partition suit at any point.

3. Application of the Limitation Act, 1963:

- While partition suits are not limited by a specific timeframe, provisions from the Limitation Act can apply when possession or title issues arise. Section 65 of the Limitation Act, for instance, imposes a 12-year limitation for suits involving the recovery of possession of immovable property based on proprietary title. This is relevant if the partition suit includes questions of ownership or rightful possession, as illustrated in Sumathi Devi (deceased) vs. Basanthi Bai (Madras) and Shub Karan Bubna @ Shub Karan Prasad Bubna vs. Sita Saran Bubna (Supreme Court). In these cases, the courts examined the co-sharers' entitlement to both ownership and possession within the 12-year limitation period.

4. Disputed Questions of Fact:

- Determining the start of the limitation period can involve complex factual issues, especially when it's unclear when a co-sharer's right was first denied. Courts typically resolve these questions only after evaluating all evidence, as seen in Tara Chand Gaur vs. Satish Chand Sharma (Delhi). The court in this case held that factual disputes, like when a co-sharer first had their rights denied, should be resolved during the final arguments stage.

5. Final Decree Applications:

- In partition suits, the case remains open until a final decree is passed, meaning there's no limitation on filing applications to finalize the decree. For example, in Sreedevi Amma vs. Nani Amma (Kerala), the court clarified that applications for final decrees could be filed over time, as the suit remains active until the entire matter is resolved.

Exceptions and Counterarguments

1. Adverse Possession:

- While a co-sharer generally has the right to seek partition anytime, they could face an adverse possession claim if another co-sharer has been in exclusive, continuous possession for an extended period. This may bar the claim of a co-sharer who has delayed asserting their rights, as seen in Vidya Devi Alias Vidya

Vati vs. Prem Prakash (Supreme Court), where adverse possession was used to contest the co-sharer's right to partition.

2. Knowledge of Prior Partition:

- If a co-sharer is aware of a previous partition and does not act within a reasonable period, their claim might be restricted by the Limitation Act principles. Courts have applied these principles, especially when there is knowledge of an earlier partition agreement, as demonstrated in R. Padmavathi (Deceased) vs. R. Govindarajulu (Deceased) (Madras). Here, the court held that a delayed response, given knowledge of an earlier partition, can prevent re-assertion of partition claims.

Conclusion

In summary, there is no strict limitation period for filing a partition suit in India, as it depends largely on the specific circumstances and the co-sharers' actions. However, issues involving ownership and possession can bring certain provisions of the Limitation Act into play, such as the 12-year limit for possession claims. Ultimately, determining the viability of a partition suit requires assessing each case's particular facts, including prior partitions and the knowledge or actions of all parties involved.

DIVIDING ASSETS? EXPLORE THE BEST WAYS TO FILE A PARTITION

In India, partitioning property can be accomplished through various methods, depending on the circumstances and the preferences of the parties involved. The three primary ways to effectuate a partition are:

1. Partition Deed

2. Family Settlement

3. Instituting a Suit

1. Partition Deed

A partition deed is a formal legal document executed by co-owners when they mutually agree to partition their property. This method is often preferred due to its simplicity and efficiency.

- Process: The co-owners negotiate the terms of the partition, and once an agreement is reached, the deed is drafted. It is executed on stamp paper and must be registered with the sub-registrar's office.

- Legal Binding: Once registered, the partition deed becomes legally binding on all parties involved.

- Contents of a Partition Deed: A well-drafted partition deed typically includes:

  - A resolution and settlement of disputes among the co-owners.

  - Defined shares allocated to each co-owner.

  - Production and acknowledgment of title deeds.

  - A comprehensive mention of all circumstances surrounding the partition.

  - Compliance with existing laws.

- Advantages: The partition deed facilitates a smooth transition of property rights and can help avoid prolonged legal battles, as it is based on mutual consent and negotiation.

2. Family Settlement

A family settlement agreement is another method of partitioning property. Unlike a partition deed, a family settlement does not require formal registration and stamping, making it a more informal yet valid approach.

- Process: Family members come together to discuss and agree on the division of property. It is essential that all parties involved sign the agreement.

- Conditions: The family settlement must be voluntary, free from coercion, fraud, or undue influence. It should aim for a fair and equitable resolution of disputes.

- Legal Status: While not formally registered, a family settlement can still hold legal weight in court, provided that it is signed by all parties and executed in good faith.

3. Instituting a Suit

When co-owners cannot agree on the terms of partition through either a deed or a family settlement, the last resort is to file a partition suit in a civil court.

- Process: A partition suit is instituted when disagreements persist, and the claimants are unable to reach a common resolution. The suit must be filed in the court that has jurisdiction over the property in question.

- Court Proceedings: In a partition suit, the court will evaluate the claims of each party, consider the evidence presented, and ultimately issue a decree to divide the property. This process can be lengthy and may involve multiple hearings.

- Legal Representation: It is advisable for claimants to engage legal counsel when filing a partition suit to ensure that their rights are adequately represented and protected throughout the legal proceedings.

Conclusion

The partition of property in India can be effectively managed through a partition deed, a family settlement, or by instituting a partition suit, depending on the circumstances. Each method has its advantages and legal implications:

- *Partition deeds offer a clear, formal resolution based on mutual agreement, while*

- *Family settlements provide a more informal approach, requiring no legal formalities but relying on the goodwill of family members.*

- *Partition suits serve as a recourse when all else fails, allowing claimants to seek a judicial resolution to their disputes.*

Understanding these methods is crucial for individuals navigating property partition issues, ensuring they choose the most suitable approach for their specific situation.

PARTITION MADE SIMPLE: STEP-BY-STEP GUIDE TO FILING YOUR SUIT IN INDIA

Filing a partition suit is the process of legally dividing property that is jointly owned, ensuring each co-owner receives their rightful share. I'll explain each step in detail, with examples, using relevant sections and orders under the Code of Civil Procedure (CPC).

Step 1: Determine Jurisdiction

1. What is Jurisdiction?

Jurisdiction is the legal authority of a court to hear and decide a case. The right court must be selected based on:

- Location of Property: File the suit where the property is located (Section 16, CPC).

- Type of Case: A civil court handles partition suits.

- Value of the Property: The value of the property determines which level of civil court (like a District Court or High Court) will hear the case.

Example: If the property is worth Rs. 20 lakh and is located in Bangalore, the suit must be filed in the Bangalore civil court that has authority over cases involving properties of that value.

Step 2: Prepare the Plaint (Order VII, CPC)

1. What is a Plaint?

A plaint is a document submitted by the person filing the suit (plaintiff), stating the details of the case and what they want from the court.

2. Key Details to Include:

 - Names and Addresses: Include the full names and addresses of all co-owners (plaintiff and defendants).

 - Cause of Action: Explain why the suit is being filed. In a partition suit, the plaintiff would state that they are a co-owner and want their share of the property.

 - Property Description: Provide a clear description, including location, size, and title information.

 - Relief Sought: State what you want the court to do, such as ordering the property to be divided equally.

Example: Ramesh files a suit saying, "I am a co-owner of a family property with my two brothers. I want my 1/3 share divided and handed over to me."

3. Verification: Ramesh must verify the plaint, confirming the truth of its contents as per Order VI, Rule 15.

Step 3: Pay Court Fee

- Why Court Fee?

Every civil suit requires a fee, which varies by state and depends on the property value. This fee must be paid for the court to process the case.

Example: If the state law requires a court fee of 1% for properties worth Rs. 10 lakh, Ramesh must pay Rs. 10,000 as a court fee.

Step 4: File the Suit (Order IV, CPC)

1. Filing:

- Submit the plaint, necessary documents, and court fee.

- The court will register the case, give it a unique case number, and schedule the first hearing.

Example: Ramesh submits his plaint along with documents like the property title, revenue records, and family tree (genealogy) proving his relationship with the other co-owners.

Step 5: Service of Summons (Order V, CPC)

1. What is a Summons?

A summons is a notice sent to the defendant (other co-owners) telling them they need to respond to the suit.

2. How Summons is Sent:

- Personal Delivery: Delivered directly to the defendant's address.

- Registered Post: Sent via mail to ensure it reaches the defendant.

- Publication in Newspaper: If the defendant can't be reached, the summons may be published in a local newspaper (Order V, Rule 20).

Example: Ramesh's brother lives in another state and is difficult to contact. The court uses both registered post and a newspaper notice to inform him.

Step 6: Filing of Written Statement by Defendant (Order VIII, CPC)

- What is a Written Statement?

The defendant replies to the plaint, presenting their side of the story and either agreeing or disagreeing with the plaintiff's claims.

Example: Ramesh's brother files a written statement, saying, "I agree that Ramesh has a 1/3 share, but I want the partition to include a specific area where I've built my house."

Step 7: Framing of Issues (Order XIV, CPC)

- What are Issues?

Issues are the questions that the court needs to resolve, based on the arguments of both parties.

Example:

- Issue 1: "Does Ramesh have a 1/3 share in the property?"

- Issue 2: "Can the property be divided by metes and bounds (physical division) without affecting any structures?"

Step 8: Collection of Evidence (Order XI & XVIII, CPC)

1. Discovery and Inspection:

Both parties may request access to each other's documents that are relevant to the case.

2. Submission of Evidence:

- Documents: Property deeds, tax records, photographs.

- Witnesses: Any individuals who can support each party's claims.

- Expert Opinions: Sometimes an architect or surveyor might be asked to give an opinion on the property division.

Example: Ramesh submits the property deed and tax records, while his brother presents witness statements claiming they had an oral agreement about the division.

Step 9: Appointment of a Commissioner for Partition (Section 75 & Order XXVI, CPC)

- Why Appoint a Commissioner?

A Commissioner, often a surveyor or an official, inspects the property to create a detailed division plan.

Example: The court appoints a Commissioner to measure the land and prepare a plan to divide it so that Ramesh and his brothers get equal parts.

Step 10: Preliminary Decree (Order XX, Rule 18, CPC)

- What is a Preliminary Decree?

The court issues a decree specifying each co-owner's share, but this does not physically divide the property yet.

Example: The court issues a preliminary decree confirming that Ramesh has a 1/3 share, his brother has another 1/3, and a third co-owner has the final 1/3.

Step 11: Apply for a Final Decree (Order XX, Rule 18(2), CPC)

- What is a Final Decree?

Once the preliminary decree is approved, a final decree is issued that actually divides the property as specified in the preliminary decree.

Example: Ramesh applies for the final decree. The court orders the property division according to the Commissioner's plan, assigning Ramesh his 1/3 share.

Step 12: Execution of Decree (Order XXI, CPC)

1. Application for Execution:

- Ramesh files for execution if the other parties do not voluntarily give him possession of his share.

2. Physical Division:

- If required, the court will arrange for an official to ensure that Ramesh's part is marked and handed over to him.

Example: The court appoints a bailiff to ensure Ramesh gets possession of his designated 1/3 portion if his co-owners do not cooperate.

Additional Considerations

1. Interim Orders:

If Ramesh is worried that his co-owners might sell parts of the property, he can apply for an injunction to prevent any sale during the suit.

2. Amendment of Pleadings:

If Ramesh discovers new facts, he can ask the court for permission to amend his plaint to include them (Order VI, Rule 17).

Conclusion

In conclusion, filing a partition suit under the Code of Civil Procedure (CPC) is a structured process designed to ensure fair division of property among co-owners or co-parceners. This process provides a legal avenue for individuals who have a rightful share in a jointly held property to claim and secure their portion through an orderly, transparent approach. Each step—from determining jurisdiction to the execution of the final decree—serves a unique purpose, safeguarding the interests of all parties involved.

The CPC outlines specific procedures to be followed at every stage, ensuring that the rights of each party are acknowledged and that there is clear evidence of ownership and entitlement. From filing the plaint with clear details and paying the appropriate court fees, to engaging in the discovery of evidence and examination by a court-appointed Commissioner, each phase brings clarity to the issues surrounding property division. The framework under CPC, including Orders and Rules, supports a methodical examination of the plaintiff's and defendant's claims, allowing for balanced consideration through written statements, issues framing, and court orders.

The preliminary and final decrees serve as critical milestones, transitioning the suit from determining ownership stakes to physically dividing the property or providing compensation, as the case may require. In addition, provisions for interim relief and amendment of pleadings protect the rights and intentions of the parties throughout the suit's duration. The ultimate execution of the decree marks the completion of this judicial process, delivering justice by ensuring each co-owner receives their lawful share or benefit.

Thus, a partition suit under CPC not only offers a comprehensive legal solution but also reinforces the principles of fairness, equity, and lawful ownership. For anyone considering or involved in a partition suit, understanding these procedural details and preparing each document meticulously can facilitate a smoother, more effective claim to their rightful property share. This process emphasizes the importance of legal structure in resolving complex family or co-ownership issues, providing a robust pathway toward clear and just outcomes.all parties are considered. Engaging a knowledgeable legal professional can significantly aid in navigating this process effectively, ensuring compliance with all legal requirements and enhancing the chances of a favorable outcome.

PARTITIONING TIME: HOW LONG DOES A SUIT REALLY TAKE?

The time required for a partition suit in India can vary greatly based on factors like the complexity of the property, number of co-owners, legal disputes, and court workload. Generally, partition suits can be time-consuming due to procedural delays and the multiple stages involved. Here's a breakdown of the time factors:

1. Initial Steps: Filing the Suit and Summons (1-3 Months)

  - Time Taken: Preparing and filing a suit typically takes around 1-3 months, depending on how soon the plaintiff files it and the court's availability.

  - Challenges: Verifying ownership documents and determining each party's share accurately can slow down filing. Additionally, court fees need to be calculated, which may require additional documentation.

2. Service of Summons and Response from Defendants (3-6 Months)

  - Time Taken: Serving summons and receiving written statements from all defendants usually takes 3-6 months.

- Challenges: Delays in serving summons to all parties, particularly if any co-owners live outside the jurisdiction or are hard to locate, can add months. Unresponsive defendants may cause adjournments, slowing the process further.

3. Framing of Issues and Evidence Collection (6-12 Months)

- Time Taken: This stage can range from 6 months to a year, as it involves framing issues, gathering evidence, and preparing for trial.

- Challenges: Gathering documentation, conducting witness examinations, and scheduling hearings often contribute to lengthy delays. Courts may grant adjournments for additional evidence, prolonging this stage.

4. Appointment of Commissioner and Property Inspection (6-12 Months)

- Time Taken: If the court appoints a commissioner for property assessment, this can add 6-12 months.

- Challenges: Commissioners may face delays in inspecting properties, particularly if multiple visits or surveys are needed. Disputes over the commissioner's report can also add time, as parties may request clarifications or file objections.

5. Preliminary Decree (6-18 Months)

- Time Taken: Issuance of a preliminary decree can take 6-18 months after evidence collection, depending on the case's complexity and backlog in the court.

- Challenges: If one party challenges the preliminary decree, the case could enter appeals, adding months or years. Parties often seek clarifications or file objections to the decree.

6. Physical Division or Sale of Property (1-2 Years)

- Time Taken: If the property can be divided, the court moves to divide it as per the shares allotted, which can take 1-2 years. If the property is sold, finding a buyer and executing the sale may also take this long.

- Challenges: Division by metes and bounds (actual physical partitioning) is challenging, especially for properties with limited divisibility. If the property is indivisible and must be sold, the sale process and division of sale proceeds can be delayed by valuation disputes or lack of consensus on the sale price.

7. Final Decree (6-12 Months)

- Time Taken: Issuing a final decree can take another 6-12 months once the division or sale of property is finalized.

- Challenges: Parties often object to the final decree's terms, file appeals, or request amendments, extending the process.

8. Execution of Decree (6-12 Months)

- Time Taken: Executing the final decree may take an additional 6-12 months, as parties might delay vacating or relinquishing their portion.

- Challenges: If any party does not comply with the decree, others can seek court intervention, but this can take several months or even years if legal resistance is encountered.

9. Appeals and Review (1-3 Years, or More)

- Time Taken: Appeals can add another 1-3 years to the timeline if parties are dissatisfied with the final decree.

- Challenges: Higher court processes are slower, and appeals or reviews are common, especially in high-value properties. Multiple rounds of appeal can extend the case's life by years.

Average Time Required for Partition Suits

On average, a simple partition suit may take 3-5 years if all parties cooperate, and the court process is straightforward. However, in more complicated cases, or those with multiple properties or contentious parties, a partition suit may take 7-10 years or more, especially if appeals and delays are involved.

Tips to Expedite Partition Suits

1. Pre-Suit Mediation: Attempt mediation or family settlements before filing a suit.

2. Efficient Documentation: Ensure all necessary documentation is complete and accurate to avoid adjournments.

3. Request for Fast-Tracking: In some cases, courts may agree to fast-track proceedings for partition suits, though this is rare.

Partition suits are known for being lengthy, and parties should be prepared for a gradual process that requires persistence and a clear legal strategy to reduce delays wherever possible.

FINAL DECREE PROCEEDINGS IN A PARTITION SUIT

In a partition suit, the final decree represents the conclusive court order that delineates each party's exact share in the disputed property and mandates its physical division according to the preliminary decree. The final decree is issued after the court determines that all procedural requirements have been fulfilled, which can involve various stages of negotiations, assessments, and possibly further hearings. Here's a comprehensive guide to understanding the final decree proceedings in a partition suit:

1. Preliminary Decree and its Role in the Final Decree

- Before a final decree can be passed, the court issues a preliminary decree to establish the rights and shares of each coparcener or family member. This preliminary decree essentially defines the roadmap for the final division, identifying who is entitled to what portion of the property but not yet executing that division.

- Only after this preliminary stage is complete does the court proceed with the final decree proceedings, during which the physical division or allotment of property occurs.

2. Application for Final Decree

- Any of the parties involved in the suit can file an application for a final decree once the preliminary decree has been issued. This application formally requests the court to conclude the partition by implementing the actual division of the property as per the terms of the preliminary decree.

- A failure by the parties to file for a final decree may result in a delay, and in some cases, a prolonged dispute if left unresolved.

3. Appointment of a Commissioner for Physical Division

- In cases where the property can be physically divided, the court often appoints a Commissioner under Order 26, Rule 13 of the Code of Civil Procedure, 1908. The Commissioner's role is to survey and partition the property on-site based on the shares defined in the preliminary decree.

- The Commissioner will inspect the property, assess its physical attributes, and prepare a detailed report outlining the feasible division that aligns with the preliminary decree. This report is then submitted to the court for review and approval.

4. Objections to the Commissioner's Report

- After the Commissioner submits their report, any party in the suit may raise objections if they believe the division is unjust or inaccurate. Common objections might include valuation discrepancies, disparities in the allocation of portions, or disputes over specific sections of the property.

- The court reviews these objections and may conduct hearings to resolve them. If necessary, the court may direct the Commissioner to revise the report or, in rare cases, appoint a new Commissioner.

5. Consideration of Indivisible Property and Sale Options

- When a property is deemed indivisible (e.g., a single house), the court may order the sale of the property and distribute the sale proceeds among the co-owners according to their entitled shares.

- Alternatively, if one of the parties wishes to retain the property, the court may allow them to do so by compensating the others with financial equivalents for their shares, maintaining fairness in the division.

6. Passing the Final Decree

- Once the court has examined the Commissioner's report and addressed any objections, it passes the final decree, which formalizes the physical division or sale of the property.

- This final decree is enforceable, meaning that each party gains independent ownership of their allocated share. The final decree can then be executed, and parties are entitled to take possession of their portions as per the decree's terms.

7. Execution of the Final Decree

- The execution of a final decree typically involves a court order of partition, through which the actual division or transfer of property rights takes place.

- If any party refuses to comply with the final decree, the court can take execution proceedings to enforce compliance. This may involve court officials physically partitioning the property, issuing instructions for sale, or imposing penalties to ensure the decree's fulfillment.

8. Impact and Binding Nature of the Final Decree

- The final decree is binding on all parties involved in the suit, including legal heirs or successors of the coparceners or family members, as well as third parties who may hold any interest in the property.

- Any appeals against the final decree must be filed promptly after the decree is issued. Delayed appeals can lead to the decree attaining finality, making it irrevocable unless challenged under extraordinary circumstances.

9. Distribution of Costs and Legal Fees

- As part of the final decree proceedings, the court may also decide on the allocation of legal costs and fees associated with the Commissioner's services. Generally, these costs are divided among the parties in proportion to their shares unless the court directs otherwise.

- In certain situations, if the court finds that a party acted in bad faith or unnecessarily prolonged the proceedings, it may impose additional costs on that party.

10. Certified Copy of the Final Decree

- After the final decree is issued, parties can obtain a certified copy from the court, which is essential for official property records, mutation, and registration in the name of the respective owners.

- A certified copy also provides parties with a legally recognized document, ensuring clear ownership and facilitating future transactions or registrations.

Conclusion

The final decree in a partition suit serves as the definitive judgment and enables parties to realize their property rights. While the process can be lengthy and intricate, especially if disputes arise during the Commissioner's assessment, the final decree ensures a fair and enforceable division, backed by legal validation. This finality prevents further conflicts and secures each party's independent control over their allocated share, achieving the ultimate aim of a partition suit: the clear division of property.

CONCLUSION

A partition suit is an essential legal remedy available to co-owners or coparceners seeking a definitive division of property when a mutual agreement cannot be reached. This process, guided by both substantive and procedural law, ensures that each claimant receives their rightful share, safeguarded by the oversight of the judiciary. While filing a partition suit requires an understanding of specific documentation, procedures, and compliance with statutory limitations, it ultimately allows family members or co-owners to settle property disputes lawfully and transparently.

The journey of a partition suit typically begins with a preliminary decree, wherein the court ascertains each party's legal rights and respective shares. This phase is crucial, as it sets the foundation for the subsequent final decree, which entails the actual division of the property. The appointment of a Commissioner to oversee the physical partition, coupled with provisions for addressing objections, ensures that the final division is equitable and practical. When direct division is not possible, alternatives like property sale or compensation maintain fairness in distributing assets.

The final decree represents the conclusive judgment, detailing each party's entitlements and making the division legally binding. The decree's enforcement can involve formal execution proceedings to ensure compliance, thus granting the parties their rightful and independent ownership. This legal finality fosters stability, preventing future disputes and solidifying property rights.

While the process can be lengthy—often spanning several years due to necessary evaluations, hearings, and potential appeals—the partition suit provides an indispensable legal path to a fair and structured division of shared property. For minors, safeguards like the appointment of a "next friend" and judicial scrutiny of their interests further reinforce the process's commitment to justice. Ultimately, a partition suit serves to transform a contentious shared asset into distinctly owned portions, enabling each co-owner or family member to exercise full rights over their share, supported by legal authority. This structured, legally sanctioned division plays a critical role in preserving familial and property harmony while protecting the interests of all involved parties.

LANDMARK SUPREME COURT JUDGMENTS ON PARTITION SUITS

The Supreme Court of India has rendered several landmark judgments on partition suits, shaping the interpretation of inheritance laws, coparcenary rights, and the role of family settlements in property division. Here are some significant judgments that have left a lasting impact on partition and property rights in India:

Prakash v. Phulavati (2015): A Comprehensive Analysis

Citation: Prakash v. Phulavati, (2016) 2 SCC 36

Court: Supreme Court of India

Bench: Justice Anil R. Dave, Justice A.K. Goel, and Justice R. Banumathi

Overview:

The Prakash v. Phulavati case is a landmark Supreme Court decision that clarified the application of the 2005 amendment to the Hindu Succession Act, 1956. This amendment significantly impacted the rights of daughters in Hindu Undivided Family (HUF) properties, making them coparceners (equal inheritors) along with sons. However, the amendment's prospective or retrospective effect had remained a subject of debate, as it affected daughters' rights in their ancestral properties. The Supreme Court, in this case, ruled that the amendment applies prospectively and not retrospectively, thereby impacting which daughters could claim coparcenary rights under the amended law.

Facts of the Case

Phulavati, the daughter of a deceased HUF member, sought to claim her share in the ancestral property as a coparcener. Her father had passed away in 1988, before the 2005 amendment to the Hindu Succession Act came into effect. After her father's death, she sought to claim equal coparcenary rights as a daughter, citing the changes introduced by the amendment. The issue was whether she could claim these rights despite her father's death preceding the amendment.

Legal Issues

1. Prospective vs. Retrospective Application: Does the 2005 amendment to the Hindu Succession Act, 1956, which grants daughters equal coparcenary rights, apply retrospectively to cases where the father passed away before the amendment?

2. Date of Enactment and Scope of Rights: What is the relevance of the father's date of death in determining the daughter's coparcenary rights in Hindu Undivided Family property?

Key Provisions Involved

- Hindu Succession Act, 1956: Initially, only male members were entitled to coparcenary rights in HUF property, meaning that sons had an automatic right to ancestral property from birth.

- Hindu Succession (Amendment) Act, 2005: Amended Section 6 to provide equal coparcenary rights to daughters, stating that a daughter of a coparcener shall, by birth, become a coparcener in her own right in the same manner as the son.

Arguments Presented

Appellant (Prakash):

1. The appellant argued that since the 2005 amendment is not explicitly retrospective, it should not apply to cases where the coparcener (the father, in this case) had died before the amendment's enactment.

2. The appellant contended that the amendment should only apply to living coparceners at the time the law was changed, aligning with the prospective nature of legislative enactments unless expressly stated otherwise.

Respondent (Phulavati):

1. The respondent argued that the amendment conferred a right by birth to daughters, similar to sons, in coparcenary property, irrespective of the date of the father's death.

2. Phulavati argued that since the amendment aimed to remove gender discrimination in ancestral property inheritance, it should be interpreted to apply to all daughters, including those whose fathers had passed away prior to 2005.

Supreme Court Decision

The Supreme Court ruled in favor of the appellant, Prakash, concluding that the 2005 amendment to the Hindu Succession Act applies prospectively and not retrospectively. The key points of the ruling were as follows:

1. Prospective Application of the 2005 Amendment:

- The Court held that for a daughter to claim coparcenary rights under the amended Act, the coparcener (father) must have been alive on the date of the amendment, i.e., September 9, 2005. Therefore, if the father passed away before this date, the daughter would not be eligible to claim coparcenary rights in the property.

- The Supreme Court emphasized that legislative intent is clear in stating that the amendment applies prospectively. Since there was no explicit provision in the amendment stating it should apply retrospectively, the amendment could not be applied to situations where the coparcener had already passed away before 2005.

2. Right by Birth Clause:

- The amendment provides daughters with coparcenary rights by birth, similar to sons. However, for this right to be actionable, the coparcener father must have been alive when the amendment took effect.

- The Court clarified that the right by birth, in this context, is dependent on the existence of the coparcener (father) on the date of the amendment. If he was not alive, the daughter would not inherit coparcenary rights.

3. Rejection of Retrospective Interpretation:

- The Court cited the legal principle that unless a statute explicitly mentions retrospective application, it is presumed to apply prospectively. Applying this principle, the Supreme Court held that the 2005 amendment did not have any retrospective impact on daughters of deceased coparceners before the amendment date.

Significance of the Judgment

The Prakash v. Phulavati judgment had far-reaching implications for daughters claiming coparcenary rights in HUF properties under the Hindu Succession Act. By clarifying the prospective nature of the 2005 amendment, the Court delineated specific guidelines on who could claim equal rights under this law. This judgment, however, led to further questions and complications, as it appeared to deny coparcenary rights to daughters whose fathers had passed away before the amendment, even though they were legally entitled as per the amended law's spirit of gender equality.

This decision was later partially reconsidered by the Supreme Court in Vineeta Sharma v. Rakesh Sharma (2020), which clarified that daughters could indeed claim coparcenary rights irrespective of whether the father was alive as of September 9, 2005. The Vineeta Sharma judgment overruled Prakash v. Phulavati, reinforcing equal coparcenary rights to daughters in all cases, thus upholding the spirit of the 2005 amendment and advancing gender equality in inheritance law.

Conclusion

Prakash v. Phulavati underscored the principle of prospective application in the absence of an express legislative statement for retrospective enforcement. While initially setting boundaries for the 2005 amendment's application, the decision led to further legal questions around gender equity in property inheritance law, which the Supreme Court addressed more broadly in Vineeta Sharma v. Rakesh Sharma. Both cases have contributed significantly to the development of coparcenary rights for daughters in India, moving progressively toward equitable treatment of sons and daughters in Hindu ancestral property rights.

VINEETA SHARMA V. RAKESH SHARMA (2020)

Key Holding: Daughters have equal coparcenary rights as sons from birth.

Summary: In a groundbreaking judgment, the Supreme Court held that daughters have an equal right to ancestral property as coparceners, just like sons, under the Hindu Succession Act, 1956 (amended in 2005). The Court clarified that a daughter's right in the property is acquired at birth, irrespective of whether the father was alive or not when the amendment came into force. This Vineeta Sharma v. Rakesh Sharma (2020): A Comprehensive Analysis

Citation: Vineeta Sharma v. Rakesh Sharma (2020) 9 SCC 1

Court: Supreme Court of India

Bench: Justice Arun Mishra, Justice S. Abdul Nazeer, Justice M.R. Shah

Overview

The Vineeta Sharma v. Rakesh Sharma case marked a significant milestone in Indian inheritance law, solidifying the equal rights of daughters to inherit ancestral property under Hindu law. This landmark judgment overruled the 2015 decision in Prakash v. Phulavati, which had restricted daughters' coparcenary rights by making them conditional upon the father's survival at the time of the 2005 amendment to the Hindu Succession Act, 1956. The Supreme Court in Vineeta Sharma ruled that daughters have equal coparcenary rights in Hindu Undivided Family (HUF) property, regardless of whether their fathers were alive when the amendment was enacted.

Background and Legal Context

The Hindu Succession Act, 1956:

- Prior to the amendment in 2005, Hindu law granted coparcenary rights (joint inheritance rights) only to male descendants in HUF property. Daughters were not considered coparceners and, therefore, had limited inheritance rights.

Hindu Succession (Amendment) Act, 2005:

- The 2005 amendment changed Section 6 of the Hindu Succession Act, 1956, providing daughters with the same rights as sons by birth in coparcenary property, effectively making them equal coparceners.

The Prakash v. Phulavati Judgment (2015):

- In this case, the Supreme Court held that the 2005 amendment would apply only if the father was alive on the amendment date, i.e., September 9, 2005. This restricted the amendment's benefits to cases where the coparcener father was living at the time of its enactment, limiting the scope of the daughter's rights.

The judgment in Prakash v. Phulavati led to inconsistencies and confusion regarding daughters' rights, particularly where the father had passed away before the amendment, prompting the need for clarification, which came with the Vineeta Sharma judgment.

Facts of the Case

Vineeta Sharma, the daughter of a deceased HUF member, sought her share in the ancestral property, asserting her rights as a coparcener under the 2005 amendment. The family disputed her claim, arguing that since their father had passed away before the amendment came into effect, she did not have coparcenary rights. The matter went to court to clarify whether the amendment could apply to daughters whose fathers had died before 2005.

Legal Issues

1. Prospective or Retrospective Application: Does the 2005 amendment apply retrospectively to daughters irrespective of the father's death before the amendment date?

2. Rights of Daughters as Coparceners: Do daughters have the right by birth to inherit property, similar to sons, under the amended Section 6 of the Hindu Succession Act?

3. Status of the 2015 Prakash v. Phulavati Decision: Should the earlier ruling in Prakash v. Phulavati, which limited daughters' rights based on the father's survival, be upheld or overruled?

Supreme Court Decision

The Supreme Court ruled in favor of Vineeta Sharma, clarifying that daughters are entitled to equal coparcenary rights, regardless of whether their fathers were alive when the amendment was enacted in 2005. The judgment effectively overruled Prakash v. Phulavati, setting a clear precedent for the equal inheritance rights of daughters in HUF property. The Court's key points were as follows:

1. Daughters Have Rights by Birth:

- The Court held that daughters are entitled to coparcenary rights by birth, similar to sons, under the Hindu Succession Act. This right is not contingent upon the survival of the father at the time of the amendment.

- Since the right is by birth, the status of the coparcener father on the amendment date has no bearing on the daughter's claim.

2. Retrospective Application of the 2005 Amendment:

- The Supreme Court clarified that the amendment applies retrospectively, allowing daughters to claim coparcenary rights even if the father had passed away before 2005.

- Although the amendment does not affect partitions that were legally and fully settled before 2005, it does grant rights to daughters for properties not formally partitioned before the amendment date.

3. Overruling Prakash v. Phulavati:

- In overruling Prakash v. Phulavati, the Court reaffirmed that statutory changes aimed at eradicating gender discrimination should be interpreted in a manner that promotes equal rights.

- The Court found that Prakash v. Phulavati had misconstrued the intent of the amendment, failing to recognize the inherent rights of daughters.

4. Undivided Coparcenary Property and Partition:

- The Court stated that coparcenary rights apply only to undivided HUF properties. If a partition was conducted and finalized under proper legal procedure before the 2005 amendment, then the amendment's provision could not re-open it.

- This means that the daughter's rights apply only to cases where no formal partition had taken place before the amendment.

Significance of the Judgment

The Vineeta Sharma judgment has a profound impact on Indian inheritance law, especially for women's rights. It reaffirms the equal status of daughters as coparceners and ensures their right to ancestral property, irrespective of their father's death before the amendment. The ruling promotes gender equality by ensuring that daughters receive the same legal standing as sons in matters of inheritance.

This decision also has far-reaching implications for pending and future cases, as it provides a uniform rule for courts to follow, ending the ambiguity left by earlier judgments. By emphasizing the retrospective application of the 2005 amendment, the Supreme Court has underscored that progressive legislation aimed at gender equality should be liberally interpreted to advance social justice.

Legal Implications of the Vineeta Sharma Judgment

1. Equal Rights in Ancestral Property:

   - The judgment ensures that daughters across India now have equal rights in HUF property, aligning with constitutional principles of gender equality.

2. No Requirement for Father's Survival:

- By removing the condition of the father's survival for daughters to claim coparcenary rights, the judgment provides clarity and removes legal impediments that previously disadvantaged daughters.

3. Limited Scope for Reopening Past Partitions:

- The Court's ruling limits the impact on cases where partitions were legally and conclusively settled before 2005. This prevents disruption of settled property arrangements while providing justice in cases where the inheritance division was incomplete.

4. Overruling Precedents:

- By overruling Prakash v. Phulavati, this judgment reinforces that laws should be interpreted in favor of inclusivity and equal rights, setting a progressive standard for future judgments on inheritance laws.

Conclusion

The Vineeta Sharma v. Rakesh Sharma judgment marks a defining moment in Indian jurisprudence, reinforcing the equal coparcenary rights of daughters in HUF property and setting a strong precedent for gender equality in property rights. By declaring the retrospective application of the 2005 amendment to the Hindu Succession Act, the Supreme Court has eliminated longstanding ambiguity around daughters' inheritance rights, ensuring they receive the same respect and recognition as sons. This judgment aligns with India's commitment to gender equality and social justice, promoting a fairer inheritance system for generations to come. judgment ensured gender equality by confirming that daughters are equal coparceners in ancestral property, with the same rights and liabilities as sons.

Significance: This decision overruled conflicting interpretations by various High Courts and earlier Supreme Court judgments. It provided clarity, affirming that daughters are entitled to seek partition of ancestral property, thus promoting gender equality in family inheritance.

GANDURI KOTESHWARAMMA V. CHAKIRI YANADI (2011): A COMPREHENSIVE ANALYSIS

Citation: Ganduri Koteshwaramma & Anr. v. Chakiri Yanadi & Anr., (2011) 9 SCC 788

Court: Supreme Court of India

Bench: Justice R.M. Lodha and Justice Jagdish Singh Khehar

Overview

The Ganduri Koteshwaramma v. Chakiri Yanadi case was a landmark judgment on daughters' rights under the Hindu Succession (Amendment) Act, 2005. This case clarified that daughters, like sons, hold coparcenary rights in Hindu Joint Family property, even if the partition process began before the 2005 amendment. The Supreme Court's ruling reinforced that daughters have equal rights in their father's property by birth, and any preliminary decree issued before the 2005 amendment does not bar their entitlement to a share in the property.

Background of the Case

The Hindu Succession Act, 1956:

- Under the original 1956 Act, daughters did not hold coparcenary rights in a Hindu Undivided Family (HUF) property, a privilege reserved for male descendants. Daughters could inherit only as legal heirs upon the death of a coparcener and did not have a birthright in ancestral property.

The Hindu Succession (Amendment) Act, 2005:

- The 2005 amendment to Section 6 of the Act granted daughters equal rights as sons in HUF property. This means daughters, by birth, became coparceners, with the same rights and liabilities in ancestral property as sons, irrespective of their father's death or survival on the amendment date.

The Issue in Ganduri Koteshwaramma's Case:

- In this case, the parties had begun a partition suit for HUF property before the 2005 amendment, and a preliminary decree was issued allocating shares without recognizing daughters as coparceners. Following the 2005 amendment, the daughters sought an equal share in the property, prompting the other parties to dispute their claim, arguing that the preliminary decree precluded further changes.

Facts of the Case

The partition suit involved the property of a Hindu Joint Family owned by the deceased coparcener, whose children included both sons and daughters. A preliminary decree had been issued, and it allocated shares solely based on the original provisions of the Hindu Succession Act, 1956, excluding daughters from a coparcenary share. When the daughters (appellants) approached the court for a modification in light of the 2005 amendment, the trial court allowed the plea, but this decision was challenged by the other coparceners (respondents).

The issue ultimately reached the Supreme Court to determine whether the daughters could claim coparcenary rights, given the 2005 amendment, even though a preliminary decree had already been issued before the amendment.

Key Issues

1. Effect of the 2005 Amendment on Pre-existing Partitions: Does the amendment granting equal coparcenary rights to daughters apply to cases where a preliminary decree had already been issued, or is it only prospective?

2. Rights of Daughters as Coparceners: Do daughters, by birth, have an inalienable right to the HUF property, and does the amendment impact ongoing proceedings?

Supreme Court's Judgment

The Supreme Court ruled in favor of Ganduri Koteshwaramma and upheld the daughters' right to coparcenary property, clarifying several legal points:

1. Retrospective Application of the Amendment:

- The Court held that the 2005 amendment has retrospective application in cases where the partition was not yet finalized. Since the decree issued was preliminary, it did not conclude the partition process, thus leaving room for the 2005 amendment to take effect.

2. Right of Daughters to Equal Shares:

- Daughters were declared equal coparceners by birth, and this right was upheld irrespective of the partition proceedings already underway. The preliminary decree was not a barrier, as the final decree had not been issued, meaning the partition process was incomplete.

- The Court emphasized that daughters have an inherent right to coparcenary property, which should be respected during partition proceedings even if they began before the amendment.

3. Preliminary Decree Not Conclusive:

- The Court differentiated between preliminary and final decrees in partition suits. It stated that a preliminary decree does not conclude the division of property, as it only decides the entitlement shares. The final decree, which effectuates partition by physically dividing the property, was yet to be passed. Thus, the daughters' coparcenary rights were enforceable even at the preliminary decree stage.

4. Effect of Section 6 Amendment:

- The amendment in Section 6 was not bound by limitations regarding the date of the father's death or the state of partition proceedings. The Court's interpretation ensured that daughters could enjoy equal rights by birth in coparcenary property, irrespective of procedural advancements before the 2005 amendment.

Significance of the Judgment

The ruling in Ganduri Koteshwaramma v. Chakiri Yanadi has substantial implications:

1. Uniformity in Daughter's Coparcenary Rights:

- This case reinforced that daughters across India are entitled to equal shares in HUF property as sons, regardless of procedural stages in partition suits. The decision brought clarity to cases where partition proceedings started before the 2005 amendment, emphasizing that daughters' rights by birth are protected regardless.

2. Retrospective Application for Justice:

- By allowing retrospective application in cases with preliminary decrees, the judgment underscored the importance of a liberal and just approach, aiming to uphold gender equality in family property rights.

3. Clarity on Decrees in Partition Suits:

- The judgment drew a clear distinction between preliminary and final decrees in partition suits, ensuring that changes in law are applied fairly until the finalization of the partition. This clarity benefits pending and future cases where similar procedural issues may arise.

4. Gender Equality in Hindu Succession:

- The case strengthened the principles of gender equality under Hindu law, aligning with progressive interpretations of the law. By upholding daughters' coparcenary rights, the ruling signaled the judiciary's support for eradicating gender discrimination in property laws.

Conclusion

The Ganduri Koteshwaramma v. Chakiri Yanadi case represents a pivotal decision in the Indian judiciary's effort to uphold gender equality in inheritance laws. By affirming daughters' coparcenary rights and clarifying the retrospective effect of the Hindu Succession (Amendment) Act, 2005, the Supreme Court ensured that daughters receive fair and equal shares in ancestral property, even in ongoing partition suits. This judgment is a cornerstone in Indian property law, harmonizing traditional Hindu laws with contemporary constitutional values of equality and justice. Through this case, the Supreme Court reiterated its commitment to addressing gender bias in property inheritance and affirmed daughters' equal legal standing in Hindu coparcenary property.

K.S. SUBBIAH PILLAI V. COMMISSIONER OF WEALTH TAX (1999): A DETAILED ANALYSIS

Citation: k.s. Subbiah pillai & others v. Commissioner of wealth tax, (1999) 4 scc 197
Court: Supreme Court of India

Bench: Justice D.P. Wadhwa, Justice S.P. Bharucha, and Justice S. Rajendra Babu

Overview

The K.S. Subbiah Pillai v. Commissioner of Wealth Tax (1999) case is a significant ruling in tax law and property inheritance within Hindu Undivided Family (HUF) structures. It primarily addressed the assessment of wealth tax on a Hindu Undivided Family and, more importantly, the impact of partial partitions within an HUF on wealth tax assessments. This case clarified that while Hindu law recognizes the right to partition family assets, such divisions must meet specific criteria to be legally and fiscally valid.

Background of the Case

Under the Hindu law, a Hindu Undivided Family (HUF) functions as a legal entity where assets are collectively owned by family members, particularly by coparceners. A coparcener is an individual who acquires a birthright to a share of the family property, including sons, daughters (post the Hindu Succession (Amendment) Act, 2005), and other descendants in line. HUFs enjoy certain tax advantages under the Wealth Tax Act, 1957, with wealth tax levied on the value of assets owned by the HUF, but it also allows for certain exemptions and deductions.

Partial Partition in HUF:

Under Hindu law, an HUF can undergo either a complete or partial partition:

- Complete Partition: The entire property and status of the HUF are divided among all family members, and the HUF ceases to exist as a legal entity.

- Partial Partition: Only a portion of the HUF's property is divided, or only some members separate from the HUF. In such cases, the HUF still exists as a legal entity with the remaining undivided members.

The Wealth Tax Act 1957 requires tax assessments for HUF assets, and a family attempting partial partition may face limitations regarding how wealth tax is applied to their assets.

Facts of the Case

1. **Partition of Property**: In this case, the family of K.S. Subbiah Pillai underwent a partial partition, where specific properties within the HUF were divided among certain family members. The partial partition was legally recognized under Hindu law but was not recognized under the Wealth Tax Act.

2. **Wealth Tax Assessment**: The Income Tax Department included the entire property of the HUF for wealth tax assessment without recognizing the effects of the partial partition. This resulted in a higher wealth tax assessment on the remaining HUF property, as the tax authorities disregarded the partial partition for tax purposes.

3. **Appeal to Wealth Tax Authorities**: K.S. Subbiah Pillai's family challenged the tax assessment, arguing that the partial partition should reduce the taxable wealth attributed to the HUF since a portion of the property was distributed to specific family members.

The core legal question was whether a partial partition in the HUF, recognized by Hindu law, should also be accepted under the Wealth Tax Act to adjust the tax liabilities of the HUF.

Key Legal Issues

1. Validity of Partial Partition under Wealth Tax Act: Whether a partial partition recognized by Hindu law should have tax implications under the Wealth Tax Act, 1957, which generally does not recognize partial partitions for adjusting wealth tax.

2. Impact on HUF's Taxable Wealth: Should the assets distributed in partial partition be excluded from the HUF's wealth tax calculation?

3. **Interpretation of Wealth Tax Act Provisions**: Specifically, Sections 20 and 21AA of the Wealth Tax Act, which address wealth tax assessments on HUFs and how partitions within an HUF affect these assessments.

Supreme Court's Judgment

The Supreme Court ruled in favor of the Commissioner of Wealth Tax, upholding that partial partitions within an HUF are not valid for wealth tax purposes unless they satisfy specific conditions set forth by the Wealth Tax Act. The court provided the following points in its judgment:

1. **Inapplicability of Hindu Law Partitions in Wealth Tax**:

- The Court ruled that the Wealth Tax Act operates independently of Hindu law concerning the taxation of HUF property. While Hindu law may allow partial partition of HUF property, such partitions are not recognized for wealth tax assessment purposes unless explicitly permitted by the Wealth Tax Act.

- The Court noted that the Wealth Tax Act has specific provisions governing HUF taxability, and these provisions do not accommodate partial partitions, aiming to prevent tax evasion or dilution of HUF tax liabilities through selective partitions.

2. Strict Interpretation of the Wealth Tax Act:

- The Court emphasized that taxation laws, particularly in areas like wealth tax, must be strictly construed. The Act's language clearly did not recognize partial partitions, which prevented families from reducing their tax burden by only partially distributing property among members.

- By following this interpretation, the Court prevented possible abuse of tax laws, ensuring that the Wealth Tax Act's intent remained intact.

3. Partial Partition as Ineffective for Tax Purposes:

- The Court held that HUFs attempting partial partition could not use it to lower wealth tax liabilities. The Wealth Tax Act was structured to consider only complete partitions that dissolve the HUF entirely, not partial transfers that merely reduce the total taxable wealth on paper without dismantling the HUF.

4. **Consistency in Taxation of HUFs**:

- Recognizing partial partitions could complicate wealth tax administration by requiring continual reassessment with every minor redistribution. The ruling simplified HUF wealth tax application by dismissing partial partitions, ensuring uniformity in tax assessment and removing scope for potential manipulations by selectively distributing assets to certain family members.

Significance of the Judgment

The K.S. Subbiah Pillai v. Commissioner of Wealth Tax case is pivotal in defining the boundaries between Hindu personal law and taxation laws in India. Its implications are far-reaching for HUFs in India and clarify the tax authorities' stance on partial partitions:

1. **Clear Distinction between Hindu Law and Tax Law:**

- The judgment reinforced that Hindu law's personal rules on partition do not automatically affect tax laws unless the legislature expressly provides for such accommodation. This separation is crucial for the consistency and effectiveness of tax assessments.

2. **Control of Wealth Tax Liabilities in HUFs:**

- By excluding partial partitions from wealth tax calculations, the Supreme Court's decision prevented families from artificially lowering their tax obligations. This ruling ensures that wealth tax applies comprehensively to all HUF assets unless the HUF completely dissolves.

3. Upholding Legislative Intent:

- The decision supports the intent behind the Wealth Tax Act, which aims to tax the full wealth of an HUF as a single entity. The ruling upheld that partial distributions of HUF wealth do not diminish the HUF's tax responsibilities.

4. Guidance for Future Cases:

- The judgment serves as a legal precedent, guiding tax authorities and courts on assessing HUF wealth under partial partition claims. It prevents HUFs from challenging wealth tax calculations on the grounds of partial partition, streamlining tax administration.

Conclusion

The Supreme Court's decision in K.S. Subbiah Pillai v. Commissioner of Wealth Tax set a crucial precedent in Indian tax law. By ruling that partial partitions of HUFs are not recognized for wealth tax assessments, the Court reinforced the Wealth Tax Act's objective of taxing the collective wealth of HUFs. This case is significant for its interpretation of tax statutes over personal law, ensuring that tax liabilities are fairly and consistently imposed on Hindu Undivided Families without dilution through selective asset distributions. The judgment remains a cornerstone in the application of tax laws to HUFs, maintaining a clear boundary between personal inheritance rights and fiscal responsibilities.

SAMPLE DRAFT OF PARTITION SUIT

IN THE COURT OF THE PRINCIPAL CITY CIVIL AND SESSIONS JUDGE AT BENGALURU

O.S. No. _____ of 20__

A.B.,

Aged about ____ years,

Son/Daughter of _____,

Resident of _____ **Plaintiff**

VERSUS

C.D.,

Aged about ____ years,

Son/Daughter of _____,

Resident of _____.

E.F.,

Aged about ___ years,

Son/Daughter of _____,

Resident of _____.   **Defendants**

MEMORANDUM OF PLAINT UNDER ORDER VII RULE 1 READ WITH SECTION 26 OF CIVIL PROCEDURE CODE

The Plaintiff submits as follows:

1. The Addresses of the parties for the purpose of service of notices and other processes from this Hon'ble court are correctly stated in the cause title, supra. The plaintiff is also care of his counsel Sri. **NS**, Advocate, near abc office Bengaluru E–Mail Phone No .

2 - The plaintiff and defendants are members of a joint Hindu family and are governed by the Hindu Succession Act, 1956. The plaintiff and defendants have an ancestral property situated at _____ (full property address) acquired through

joint family earnings. The property has not been partitioned, and all parties have a right to claim their respective shares.

3. The schedule property, forming part of this suit for partition, is more specifically described as follows:

   - Schedule Property: _____ (provide brief description of the property, including any unique identifiers such as survey number, extent, and boundaries).

4. The plaintiff and defendants have been in joint possession of the property. However, due to disagreements and an inability to use the property equitably, the plaintiff has been deprived of their rightful share. Despite repeated requests, the defendants have refused to partition the property amicably.

5. The plaintiff has a legitimate right to an equal share of the schedule property. The refusal by the defendants to allow the plaintiff to enjoy the property or to formally partition it has caused mental and financial hardship to the plaintiff.

6. Since the defendants are not inclined to settle the matter amicably, the plaintiff is compelled to approach this Hon'ble Court for a decree of partition.

PRAYER

Wherefore, the plaintiff prays that this Hon'ble Court may be pleased to:

a. Pass a preliminary decree declaring the plaintiff's right, title, and interest in the schedule property and grant a share in the property as may be appropriate under the Hindu Succession Act, 1956.

b. Order for partition and separate possession of the plaintiff's share in the schedule property.

d. Grant such other and further relief as this Hon'ble Court deems fit in the interest of justice and equity.

Bengaluru

Dated this the ___ day of _____, 20__.

SCHEDULE

Item No.1

All the piece and parcel of the property bearing sy.no   totally measuring guntas including   guntas of kharab land situated at yelahanka ,Bengaluru

East by:

West by:

North by:

South by:

<u>VERIFICATION</u>

I, A.B., the plaintiff in the above suit, do hereby solemnly affirm and declare that the contents of paragraphs 1 to 6 in the plaint are true and correct to the best of my knowledge, information, and belief.

Place:

Date: Plaintiff